P9-DXI-597

FLORIDA

The Sunshine State

BY
JOHN HAMILTON

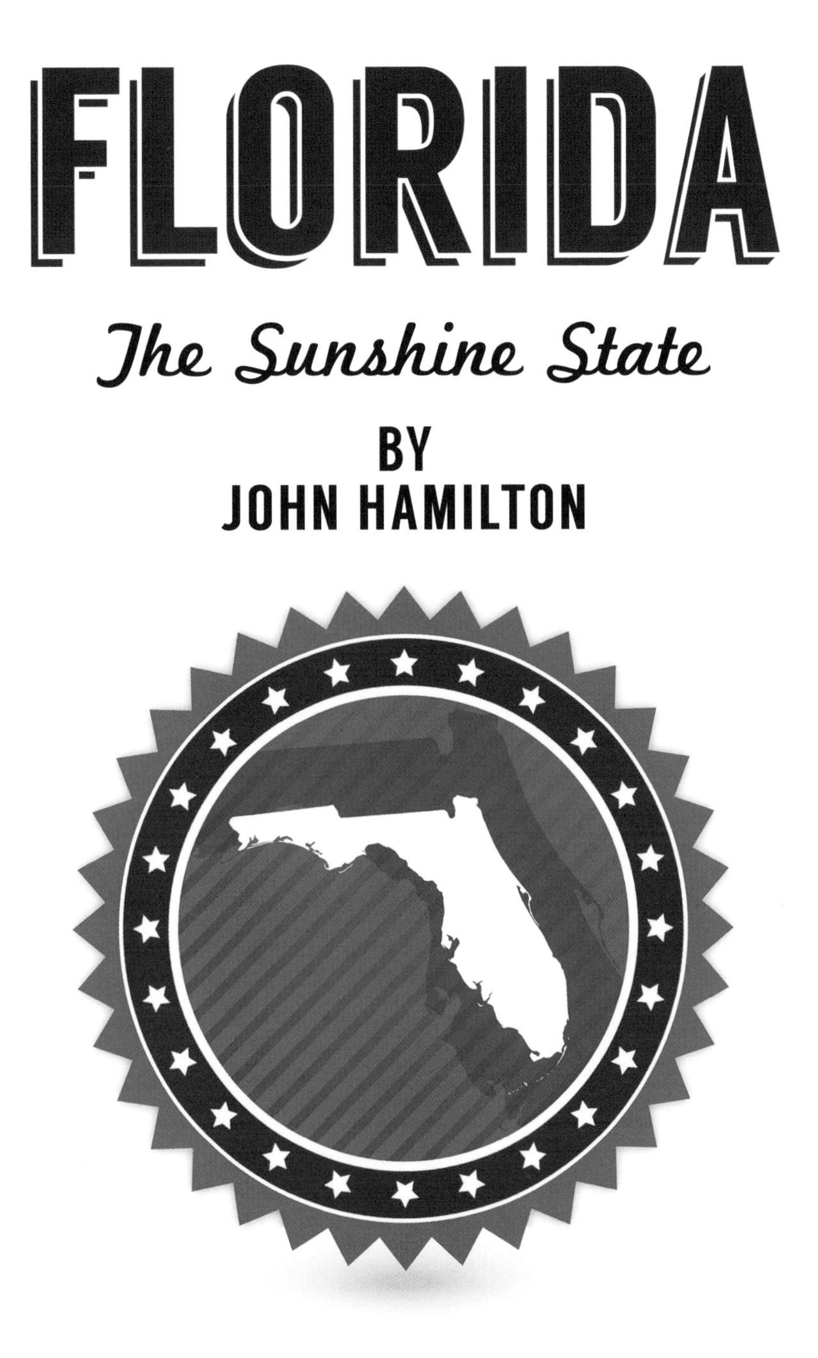

Abdo & Daughters
An imprint of Abdo Publishing | abdopublishing.com

abdopublishing.com

Published by ABDO Publishing, a division of ABDO, PO Box 398166, Minneapolis, Minnesota 55439.

Printed in the United States of America, North Mankato, Minnesota.
012016
092016

THIS BOOK CONTAINS RECYCLED MATERIALS

Editor: Sue Hamilton **Contributing Editor:** Bridget O'Brien
Graphic Design: Sue Hamilton
Cover Art Direction: Candice Keimig **Cover Photo Selection:** Neil Klinepier
Cover Photo: iStock
Interior Images: Alamy, AP, Busch Gardens, Corbis, Florida Dept of Environmental Protection, Florida Fish & Wildlife Conservation Commission, Florida Panthers, Getty, Glow, Granger, History in Full Color-Restoration/Colorization, iStock, Jacksonville Jaguars, John Hamilton, Library of Congress, Miami Dolphins, Miami Heat, Miami Marlons, Mile High Maps, NASA, Niels Proctor-University of Florida, NOAA-Johnathon McCauley, Orlando City Soccer Club, Orlando Magic, RavenFire Media, SeaWorld, Tampa Bay Buccaneers, Tampa Bay Lightning, Tampa Bay Rays, U.S. Marines, Walt Disney World Orlando, Wikimedia.

Statistics: *State and City Populations*, U.S. Census Bureau, July 1, 2014 estimates; *Land and Water Area*, U.S. Census Bureau, 2010 Census, MAF/TIGER database; *State Temperature Extremes*, NOAA National Climatic Data Center; *Climatology and Average Annual Precipitation*, NOAA National Climatic Data Center, 1980-2015 statewide averages; *State Highest and Lowest Points*, NOAA National Geodetic Survey.

Websites: To learn more about the United States, visit booklinks.abdopublishing.com. These links are routinely monitored and updated to provide the most current information available.

Cataloging-in-Publication Data

Names: Hamilton, John, 1959- author.
Title: Florida / by John Hamilton.
Description: Minneapolis, MN : Abdo Publishing, [2016] | The United States of America | Includes index.
Identifiers: LCCN 2015957509 | ISBN 9781680783117 (print) | ISBN 9781680774153 (ebook)
Subjects: LCSH: Florida--Juvenile literature.
Classification: DDC 975.9--dc23
LC record available at http://lccn.loc.gov/2015957509

CONTENTS

The Sunshine State. 4
Quick Facts 6
Geography 8
Climate and Weather 12
Plants and Animals. 14
History. 18
Did You Know? 24
People 26
Cities 30
Transportation 34
Natural Resources. 36
Industry 38
Sports. 40
Entertainment 42
Timeline. 44
Glossary 46
Index 48

THE SUNSHINE STATE

Florida has a long and colorful history. The town of St. Augustine was settled in 1565, decades before the English founded Jamestown in Virginia, or the Puritans landed in Massachusetts. Early Spanish settlers discovered what Native Americans already knew: Florida is a land of tropical beauty, with abundant natural resources and warm weather that lasts throughout the year. Its pleasant climate is why it is today called "The Sunshine State."

Florida remembers its historical roots, but its modern cities bustle with activity. The state attracts older people who want to relax, but it is also a magnet for the young, with its many amusement parks and sandy beaches. Fiery space rockets compete for attention with the wildlife-filled Everglades wilderness. All this activity is tied together by the state's melting pot of diverse people, who sway to a Latin American beat.

People enjoy the Calle Ocho Latin street festival held every year in Miami, Florida.

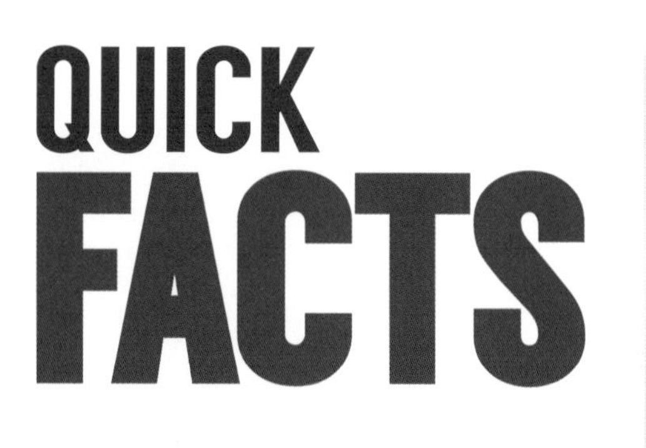

Name: Explorer Juan Ponce de León named the land *la Florida*, after the Spanish Easter celebration "feast of the flowers."

State Capital: Tallahassee, population 188,107

Date of Statehood: March 3, 1845 (27th state)

Population: 19,893,297 (3rd-most populous state)

Area (Total Land and Water): 65,758 square miles (170,312 sq km), 22nd-largest state

Largest City: Jacksonville, population 853,382

Nickname: The Sunshine State

Motto: In God We Trust

State Bird: Mockingbird

State Flower: Orange Blossom

State Rock: Agatized Coral

Agatized Coral

State Tree: Sabal Palm

State Song: "Old Folks at Home"

Highest Point: Britton Hill, 345 feet (105 m)

Sabal Palm

Lowest Point: Atlantic Ocean and Gulf of Mexico, 0 feet (0 m)

Average July High Temperature: 92°F (33°C)

Record High Temperature: 109°F (43°C), in Monticello on June 29, 1931

Average January Low Temperature: 46°F (8°C)

Record Low Temperature: -2°F (-19°C), in Tallahassee on February 13, 1899

Average Annual Precipitation: 53 inches (135 cm)

Number of U.S. Senators: 2

Number of U.S. Representatives: 27

U.S. Postal Service Abbreviation: FL

GEOGRAPHY

Florida is the southernmost of the 48 contiguous states. (Only Hawaii is farther south.) Most of the state is a large peninsula that juts southeast, between the Atlantic Ocean and the Gulf of Mexico. North of Florida are the states of Alabama and Georgia. Florida has 8,426 miles (13,560 km) of shoreline, second only to Alaska.

Northwestern Florida is called the Panhandle. Florida's northern region has more hills than the flatlands of the south. However, even Florida's highest spot, Britton Hill, is only 345 feet (105 m) above sea level. Florida has the lowest "high" point of any state.

Key West, Florida, has a concrete marker indicating the southernmost point in the continental United States. It is a popular spot for tourists to take photos.

Florida's total land and water area is 65,758 square miles (170,312 sq km). It is the 22nd-largest state. The state capital is Tallahassee.

Most of southern Florida is flat. In many areas, the elevation is barely above sea level. The Everglades are at the southern tip of the peninsula. It is a region of swamps and marshes. It teems with wildlife. Everglades National Park protects the very southern edge of this important ecosystem.

South of the Florida mainland is a string of islands. They stretch in a crescent shape to the southwest, into the Gulf of Mexico. The islands are called the Florida Keys. Popular tourist destinations, they are connected by a highway and several spectacularly long bridges. The last inhabited island in the chain is Key West. It is the most southern point in the contiguous United States. It is only about 90 miles (145 km) from the island nation of Cuba. Between Florida and Cuba are the Straits of Florida.

Everglades National Park is a huge area that spans 1.5 million acres (607,028 ha) of Florida's southern tip. Wildlife fills its swamps and marshes, including American alligators, crocodiles, frogs, panthers, storks, herons, and egrets.

Sanibel Island is one of about 4,500 islands that are just off Florida's coast. The beautiful white sand beaches draw many tourists.

Florida has about 7,700 lakes, 663 miles (1,067 km) of beaches, and hundreds of rivers and streams. There are dozens of natural springs that bubble up from underground lakes. The Saint Johns River is the state's longest. It is 273 miles (439 km) long. Off Florida's coast are about 4,500 islands.

Florida's biggest lake is Lake Okeechobee, northwest of Miami. It covers about 700 square miles (1,813 sq km). Its average depth is only 9 feet (3 m). The lake is an important source of water for the Everglades.

CLIMATE AND WEATHER

Most of Florida has a subtropical climate. The southern tip is tropical. The weather is usually warm and humid. Breezes from the nearby Atlantic Ocean and Gulf of Mexico keep temperatures from getting too hot. In July, the average high temperature is 92°F (33°C). The hottest temperature ever recorded in the state was 109°F (43°C), on June 29, 1931, in the town of Monticello. In January, the average low temperature is 46°F (8°C). The coldest temperature ever experienced in Florida happened on February 13, 1899, in Tallahassee. On that day, the thermometer dipped to -2°F (-19°C). Such cold weather is very rare. In the Florida Keys, frost has never been seen as long as weather scientists have been keeping records.

Even though Florida's nickname is "The Sunshine State," thunderstorms frequently rumble overhead. The state's average rainfall is 53 inches (135 cm) per year. Summer months get the most rain.

A lightning strike near Satellite Beach, Florida.

Dangerous hurricanes sometimes strike Florida. These large, powerful storms form in the Atlantic Ocean. When Florida is in a hurricane's path, great damage and loss of life can occur.

Hurricanes, with sustained winds of at least 74 mph (119 kph), sometimes blow in from the Atlantic Ocean or Gulf of Mexico to strike Florida's coastline.

PLANTS AND ANIMALS

Florida is rich with plants and wildlife, thanks to its mild climate, different soil types, and closeness to the ocean. Many thousands of kinds of plants grow in Florida, including hundreds of species of wildflowers and grasses. Saw grass gets its name from the saw-like teeth that line its edges.

Saw Grass Close-Up

Forests cover about half the state. Most of the timberlands are in the north. Statewide, there are about 17 million acres (6.9 million ha) of forests. Almost half of all United States tree species can be found in Florida.

Common conifers include pine (shortleaf, longleaf, spruce, and loblolly), bald cypress, and pond cypress. Some of the many common hardwoods include red maple, hickory, ash, magnolia, sweet gum, elm, plus many varieties of oak. The most common palm tree is the cabbage palm, also called the sabal palmetto. It can grow up to 65 feet (20 m) high. It is the official state tree of Florida.

Saw grass forms a "river of grass" in the Everglades.

There are more than 500 species of birds living in Florida. They include turkeys, eagles, hawks, owls, and doves. Many birds live near water. They include gulls, egrets, sandpipers, ducks, herons, pelicans, ibises, and roseate spoonbills. Many people think of American flamingoes when they visit southern Florida, but these pink, long-legged birds are rare in the wild. They are more common in Central and South America, and in the islands of the Caribbean Sea.

Heron

Common Florida land animals include raccoons, skunks, bobcats, black bears, armadillos, foxes, and deer. The tiny Key deer is an endangered type of white-tailed deer. It lives in the Florida Keys. The Florida panther, or puma, is Florida's official state animal. Less than 180 remain in the wild.

Florida's freshwater wetlands are home to many American alligators. These reptiles can exceed 10 feet (3 m) in length and weigh more than 1,000 pounds (454 kg). Rare American crocodiles are found in the Everglades. They are similar to alligators, but have narrower snouts and can live in salty estuary water. Other Florida reptiles include turtles, geckos, skinks, and anoles. There are more than 40 species of snakes. They include poisonous rattlesnakes, water moccasins, copperheads, and coral snakes.

Swimming in Florida's many lakes and offshore waters are hundreds of species of fish. Largemouth bass are prized by anglers. Aquatic mammals include bottlenose dolphins, porpoises, and manatees.

HISTORY

People lived in Florida long before Europeans discovered the New World. The first people were called Paleo-Indians. They were the ancestors of today's Native Americans. They arrived in Florida at least 12,000 years ago. They mainly hunted and fished.

When the first European explorers landed in Florida in the 1500s, they found a land inhabited by several hundred thousand Native Americans. They were members of many tribes. Some of the biggest groups included the Calusa, Timucua, Apalachee, Ais, Tocobaga, and Tequesta people.

Native Americans fish in the 1500s.

Juan Ponce de León

Juan Ponce de León from Spain sailed to Florida in 1513. He landed along the east coast, south of today's city of St. Augustine. He named the new area *La Florida*, which in Spanish means "flowery land." The land was filled with tropical plants. Also, the explorers landed during the Easter season. The Spanish called this time *Pascua Florida*, the "Festival of Flowers."

Juan Ponce de León returned to Florida in 1521. It is a myth that he was looking for the fabled fountain of youth. He and his men came to claim land for Spain and find gold and other riches.

Hernando de Soto's expedition lands at Tampa Bay, Florida, in 1539.

Over the next several decades, explorers from Spain and France tried building settlements in Florida. Pánfilo de Narváez from Spain arrived in 1528. Hernando de Soto, also from Spain, landed in 1539. Both expeditions were unsuccessful. Another Spanish colony was destroyed by a hurricane in 1561.

In 1564, French Huguenots created a settlement called Fort Caroline. It was near today's city of Jacksonville. The settlers were massacred by the Spanish, who feared French competition.

The city of St. Augustine was founded by Spanish settlers in 1565. Today, it is the oldest continuously settled town in the United States.

For almost 250 years, the European superpowers of Spain, France, and Great Britain fought to control Florida. During this time, many of Florida's Native Americans were killed by disease and warfare, or were sold into slavery. By the mid-1700s, most of the native tribes were wiped out.

Other Native Americans, many from the Creek tribe, migrated south from Georgia, Alabama, and South Carolina. Together with escaped African American slaves, these newcomers were called *Cimarrónes*. The word means "wild" or "untamed" in Spanish. They later became known as the Seminole people. They were a powerful force in Florida.

In 1821, Spain gave up Florida to the United States. Settlers wanted more land to grow crops such as cotton. After several wars with the Seminole people in the mid-1800s, the United States Army finally forced most of them to move to a reservation in faraway Oklahoma.

United States Marines search for Native Americans among the mangroves during Florida's Second Seminole War from 1835-1842. The Seminoles fought fiercely to protect their land, but ultimately were forced to move.

Florida became the 27th state in 1845. Just a few years later, in 1861, it left the Union to join the Southern Confederacy. The Southern states were for slavery. The North wanted to abolish slavery and keep the United States together. Most of the battles in the Civil War happened in states to the north. However, some Florida coastal cities were captured by Union soldiers.

Before the Civil War, Florida's economy relied mainly on cotton plantations and small farms. After the war ended in 1865, the economy began to change. In 1881, phosphate was discovered in Florida. This valuable mineral is used in cattle feed and fertilizer. The lumber industry also grew in the 1880s.

Starting in the 1880s, railroads were built connecting Florida to states in the north. Moving products and people became much easier and faster. Businesses grew, and so did the state's population.

A Florida Southern Railway train at a station in Punta Gorda, Florida.

Florida's population boomed in the 1920s.

Florida's population continued to boom in the 1920s. The tourism industry grew. Many vacationers liked the state so much they decided to buy land in sunny Florida. In the 1940s, during and after World War II, new United States military bases helped build Florida's economy.

Florida continues to grow today. Businesses like the state's closeness to the Caribbean region. People seeking nice weather come from northern states. Many people also come from Latin America, especially the Caribbean.

Immigrants from Cuba, Haiti, and Colombia give many parts of Florida a very international flavor. The state has such a large Latino population that in some places Spanish is spoken more than English. Florida is a place of many cultures and opportunities.

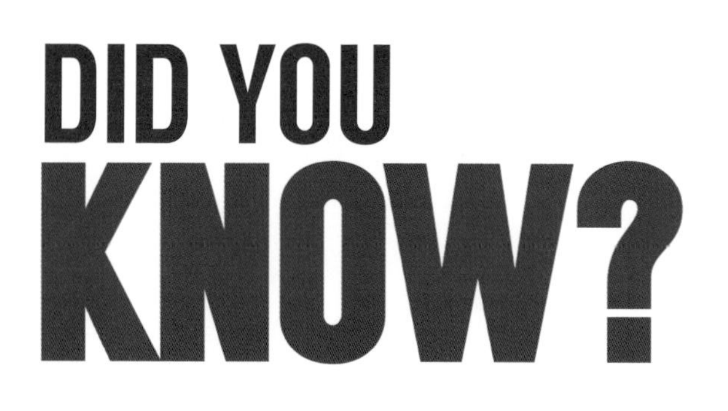

- One of the first popular sunscreens was invented by a Florida pharmacist. In 1944, Benjamin Green developed Red Vet Pet, which he made for U.S. Army troops needing sun protection. The sunscreen was later refined and sold by the Coppertone company.

- Burmese pythons are an invasive snake species recently found in south Florida. Many have made their home in the Everglades after being released into the wild by thoughtless pet owners. These large constrictors feed on native birds and animals. They are not the only invasive species threatening this fragile ecosystem. Florida also has wild hogs. They are destructive and can carry disease.

- More than 16 million bricks were used to build Fort Jefferson, which is located on a small island in the Dry Tortugas. Starting in 1846, construction lasted almost 20 years. The Dry Tortugas is a group of small islands in the Gulf of Mexico about 70 miles (113 km) west of Key West. Fort Jefferson was used as a base by the United States military. Today, it is part of Dry Tortugas National Park.

Castillo de San Marcos National Monument

- The city of St. Augustine is the oldest continuously settled non-Native American city in the United States. It was founded by Spanish settlers in 1565. St. Augustine is located in the northeast corner of Florida, along the Atlantic Ocean coast. The city was the capital for more than 200 years when Spain controlled Florida. Today, St. Augustine has a population of about 13,000. It is a popular tourist destination because of its many historical Spanish-style buildings and museums. These include Castillo de San Marcos National Monument, Fort Matanzas National Monument, and St. Augustine Alligator Farm Zoological Park.

- Florida is called "The Lightning Capital of the United States." It has the most lightning strikes of any state. Thunderstorms form over Florida about 100 days each year. Most of Florida is between the warm waters of the southern Atlantic Ocean and the Gulf of Mexico. High heat and humidity combine to form thunderstorms, which bring frequent lightning. Each year in the United States, about 100 people are killed by lightning strikes. On average, between 10 and 13 of those deaths happen in Florida. The most dangerous time of year is between late May and late September.

Osceola (1804-1838) was a war chief of the Florida Seminole American Indians. He was born in Alabama. His father was an English trader and his mother was a Creek Native American. Osceola and his mother migrated to Florida, where they joined the Seminoles. In 1835, Osceola began fighting against the United States government. Soldiers tried to force the Seminoles off their land and move them to a reservation far to the west in Oklahoma. Osceola gathered a band of Seminoles and runaway slaves and fought U.S. troops for almost two years. After attacking, they always managed to escape into the thick Everglades wilderness. Finally, in 1837, Osceola attended a peace conference. He was arrested and then imprisoned at Fort Moultrie in South Carolina. He died a few months later, probably because of malaria. Osceola's betrayal caused an uproar across the country. Today, many landmarks are named in his honor, including a county and national forest in Florida.

Marjory Stoneman Douglas (1890-1998) was a writer and tireless defender of the Florida Everglades. She is often called the "Mother of the Everglades." She was born in Minneapolis, Minnesota, but spent her adult life in Florida. She worked for the *Miami Herald* newspaper and also wrote books and short stories. She was passionate about saving the delicate Everglades ecosystem from land developers. Her most famous book was *The Everglades: River of Grass*. It was published in 1947, the same year Everglades National Park opened. Her book included these famous words: "There are no other Everglades in the world… Nothing anywhere else is like them…" She was awarded the Presidential Medal of Freedom in 1993, at the age of 103.

Jacqueline Cochran (1906-1980) was a skilled pilot who held more speed, altitude, and distance records than anyone else before her. She competed in air races in the 1930s, at a time when most pilots were men. During World War II, she trained hundreds of women to fly non-combat missions for the U.S. military. In 1953, she became the first woman to break the sound barrier. Cochran was born near Pensacola, Florida.

Sidney Poitier (1927-) is an Academy Award-winning actor and director. He was the first African American man to be nominated for an Academy Award, for his 1958 role in *The Defiant Ones*. He was the first African American man to win an Oscar, for his 1963 performance in *Lilies of the Field*. His most popular roles were in *Guess Who's Coming to Dinner* (1967), *In the Heat of the Night* (1967), and *To Sir, With Love* (1967). Poitier was born in Miami, Florida.

Gloria Estefan (1957-) is a Grammy Award-winning singer and songwriter. She has sold more than 100 million records worldwide. She was born in Cuba, but her family fled to Miami, Florida, when she was a baby. They joined the many thousands of people who left Communist Cuba and settled in Florida.

Estefan's band was called Miami Sound Machine. She sang lead vocal. The band's music blended traditional Latin American music with dance and pop. Her first big hit was "Conga," in 1985. She went on to create many hit singles and best-selling albums. In 1989, she continued her career as a solo artist. Today, she is known as the "Queen of Latin Pop." She has won seven Grammys, and was awarded the Ellis Island Congressional Medal of Honor. She has also made many stage, film, and television appearances. In addition, she is a children's book writer, and owns several Cuban-themed restaurants in Florida.

CITIES

Tallahassee is the capital of Florida. It is in the northwestern part of the state, in the Panhandle region. It has a population of 188,107. Tallahassee is a center for agriculture and scientific research. It is also home to law firms and trade associations. State and city governments are top employers, along with hospitals and medical centers. The city has a small-town atmosphere. It hosts Florida State University, Florida A&M University, and Tallahassee Community College. There are many museums, parks, and festivals in Tallahassee. The Red Hills Horse Trials is a world-famous equestrian competition held each year.

Miami isn't the largest city in Florida, but many people think it is the most interesting. It has a population of 430,332. That number swells to about 5.5 million counting the surrounding cities and towns. Miami is a center of business and banking. It also has a thriving arts and entertainment industry. Many different people mix to create multicultural communities. More than two-thirds of the people come from Latin American countries, many from Cuba and Haiti. Modern downtown skyscrapers mix with art deco buildings of the 1930s painted in pastel pinks and aquas. Tourism is a big part of the city's economy. Miami is often called the "Cruise Ship Capital of the World."

Jacksonville is Florida's largest city. Located in the state's northeastern corner, it has a population of 853,382. This large, sprawling city is home to many major banks and insurance companies. Import businesses trade in goods such as automobiles and coffee. The city also hosts large shipyards. It has the largest deepwater port in the South, and several military bases. The U.S. military is the city's largest employer. Jacksonville is a major transportation hub. It is connected to other regions by a large network of seaports, railways, airports, and interstate highways. Many colleges are located in the city, including the University of North Florida and Jacksonville University.

Tampa is on the west coast of Florida, near the Gulf of Mexico. It rests along an inlet of water called Tampa Bay. Other cities nestled along Tampa Bay include St. Petersburg and Clearwater. Together, this large metro area has a population of about 3 million. Within Tampa's city limits are 358,699 people. The city has a large port that handles cargo and cruise ships. Health care, finance, and tourism are all important industries. The Museum of Science & Industry and Busch Gardens are major tourist attractions. Tampa has many theaters, concert halls, nightclubs, and museums. The city is famous for its Cuban sandwiches and other ethnic foods. The Gasparilla Pirate Festival has brought an invasion of dress-up pirates to the city each year since 1904.

TRANSPORTATION

Florida has about 122,000 miles (196,340 km) of roadways that crisscross the state. Interstate 10 travels east and west across north Florida. Interstate 4 goes northeast and southwest across the middle of the state. Interstates 75 and 95 travel mainly north and south. At the city of Naples, Interstate 75 cuts to the east, crossing over to Fort Lauderdale. This part is often called "Alligator Alley."

U.S. Route 1 is known as the Overseas Highway. It connects the mainland with the Florida Keys. These islands stretch to the southwest, into the Gulf of Mexico. Forty-two bridges were built starting in the 1930s, the longest of which is almost seven miles (11 km) long. The total length of the highway is 113 miles (182 km), ending at Key West.

U.S. Route 1, known as the Overseas Highway, connects Miami with Key West, Florida. Beside the highway are parts of the Overseas Railroad, which was partially destroyed by a hurricane in 1935. Both the highway and what's left of the railroad are on the U.S. Register of Historic Places.

Cruise ships line up at the Port of Miami.

Florida has 14 deepwater seaports for large cargo vessels and cruise ships. The busiest include Port Miami, Port Everglades, Port of Jacksonville, and Port Tampa Bay. Together, Florida seaports move about 100 million tons (90.7 million metric tons) of cargo and more than 14 million cruise passengers each year.

Miami International Airport is one of the busiest airports in the United States. From there, many travelers continue to islands in the Caribbean or South America. Other busy Florida airports include Orlando International, Tampa International, Palm Beach International, and Fort Lauderdale-Hollywood International Airports.

Planes load and unload passengers at Miami International Airport. It has more than 80 airlines, which travel to about 150 destinations around the world.

NATURAL RESOURCES

Although most tourists don't realize it, vast amounts of Florida land are used for farming, ranching, and forestry. There are about 47,500 commercial farms in Florida, covering almost 10 million acres (4 million ha) of land. Agriculture is the state's second-biggest industry. Florida's farms are located mainly in the north and central parts of the state. They grow more than 250 kinds of fruits and vegetables, which are exported to more than 140 countries worldwide. The most valuable products are oranges, greenhouse plants, tomatoes, dairy, and sugarcane.

Florida has about 47,500 commercial farms with a wide variety of crops.

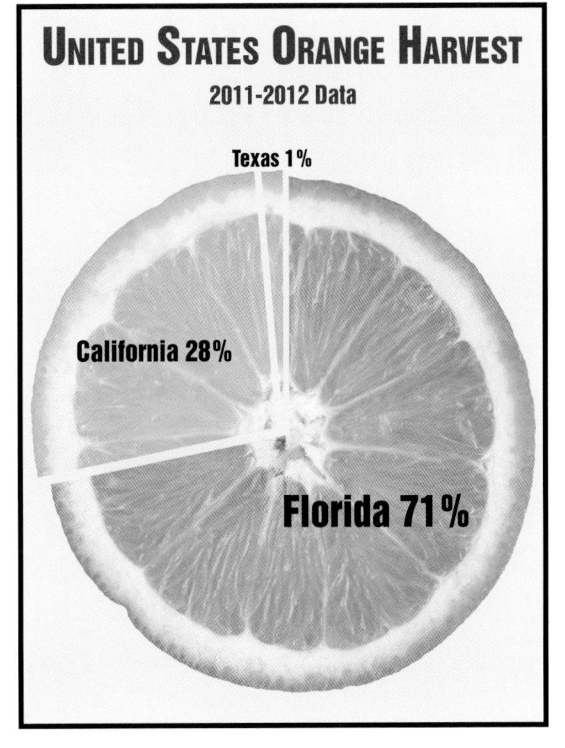

Most of Florida has fine, sandy soil. Combined with a sunny climate and no freezing temperatures, the state is perfect for growing citrus fruits such as oranges and grapefruits. Florida produces more than two-thirds of the country's citrus fruits. Oranges are the state's number one crop.

Florida's forests are harvested for wood products, mainly in the northern part of the state. Grasslands in south-central Florida are used to graze cattle.

Minerals mined in Florida include titanium, limestone, and pure silica sand. A very important mineral is phosphate. It is found in west-central Florida. It is used to make many products, including fertilizer used by farmers, livestock feed supplements, lightbulbs, and toothpaste. Florida produces about 65 percent of the United States's phosphate supply.

Railroad cars take Florida-mined phosphate rock to a fertilizer plant.

INDUSTRY

Tourism is Florida's biggest industry. Almost 100 million tourists from all over the world visit Florida each year. They add more than $67 billion to the state's economy. They come to enjoy the warm climate and sandy beaches, especially in winter. They also flock to the state's many large amusement parks, such as Walt Disney World Resort, Universal Orlando Resort, Busch Gardens, and SeaWorld. They come for sporting events, fine dining, and shopping. The growth of Florida's tourism industry has helped other businesses, such as restaurants, transportation, and construction.

Agriculture continues to be a big state employer. Service industries, such as banking and insurance, help the state's economy. Manufacturing isn't as big as in other states, but some industries are important. They include food processing (such as orange juice), printing, computers, transportation equipment, and wood products. Construction companies are often kept busy repairing damage after storms pummel the state.

Florida has several large military bases. They provide many jobs. Cape Canaveral's John F. Kennedy Space Center occupies 219 square miles (567 sq km) of land on the east coast near the city of Titusville. It is a major spaceport where rockets are launched. The space industry brings in more than $4.1 billion to Florida's economy.

NASA's Kennedy Space Center brings in billions of dollars to Florida.

SPORTS

With so many people living in Florida, the state is fortunate to have several major league teams. National Football League teams include the Miami Dolphins, the Jacksonville Jaguars, and the Tampa Bay Buccaneers. Florida often hosts the Super Bowl, thanks to its warm climate.

The Miami Heat and Orlando Magic play for the National Basketball Association. Florida's Major League Baseball teams include the Miami Marlins and the Tampa Bay Rays. Many teams play in Florida during spring training. The Tampa Bay Lightning and Florida Panthers play in the National Hockey League. Orlando City SC is a Major League Soccer team.

The famous Daytona 500 is a 500-mile (805-km) NASCAR race held every year at Daytona International Speedway in Daytona Beach, Florida. Daytona International Speedway is the largest outdoor stadium in Florida.

Florida has many college sports teams from cities such as Miami, Tampa, Tallahassee, and Jacksonville. During the New Year holiday, college football plays a postseason game at the Orange Bowl in Miami Gardens. The Orange Bowl has been played annually for more than 80 years.

Daytona International Speedway is a multi-layout track that hosts several racing events, including NASCAR's Daytona 500. It is one of the biggest races in the country. It is part of the Sprint Cup Series of stock car races, held each year in Daytona Beach.

Outdoor sports are big in Florida. Many people flock to the state's warm climate to enjoy swimming, boating, deep-sea and freshwater fishing, diving, and golf.

ENTERTAINMENT

Florida is famous for its large amusement parks. Walt Disney World Resort near Orlando is one of the biggest tourist destinations in the world. More than 50 million people visit each year to enjoy rides and activities in the Magic Kingdom, Epcot, Hollywood Studios, Animal Kingdom, plus water parks and golf courses.

At Universal Orlando Resort, visitors can go on movie-themed rides, including the Wizarding World of Harry Potter. At SeaWorld Orlando, many ocean creatures are on display, including dolphins, sharks, and orcas. Tampa's Busch Gardens features thrill rides and open-air tours where visitors can watch African animals. The John F. Kennedy Space Center near Titusville is also a popular tourist destination.

Walt Disney World's Magic Kingdom is the most visited theme park in the world. In 2014, it averaged about 53,000 visitors a day.

Florida's cities are filled with world-class symphonies, museums, and art galleries. There are many historical sites to visit. Key West is an island town at the end of U.S. Route 1. Attractions include a lighthouse built in 1847, Nobel Prize-winning writer Ernest Hemingway's house, the Key West Aquarium, and the Mel Fisher Maritime Museum, where visitors can see gold and silver treasure recovered from sunken Spanish galleons.

For outdoor lovers, Florida hosts three national parks, including Everglades, Biscayne, and Dry Tortugas National Parks. The state also has more than 100 state parks, and many national monuments and seashores.

10,000 BC—Native Americans live in the area that will become Florida.

1513—Ponce de León's first visit to Florida.

1521—Ponce de León's second visit. Native Americans stop him from settling in the area.

1539—Hernando de Soto lands in Florida.

1565—The city of St. Augustine is founded.

1845—Florida becomes the 27th state.

1861—Florida leaves the Union and joins the Confederacy. The Civil War begins.

1880s—Railroads begin to connect Florida with the rest of the United States.

1920s—People rush to claim land in Florida.

1962—NASA builds the Launch Operations Center on Florida's east coast. It is later renamed the Kennedy Space Center.

1971—Walt Disney World Resort opens with the Magic Kingdom theme park.

1973 & 1974—The Miami Dolphins win back-to-back Super Bowl championships.

1981—*Columbia* is the first space shuttle launched from Kennedy Space Center.

2003—The Tampa Bay Buccaneers win the Super Bowl. The Florida Marlins win the World Series.

2006—The Miami Heat wins its first NBA Finals championship series.

2011—The space shuttle *Atlantis* lifts off from Cape Canaveral. It is the last space shuttle mission.

Anoles
A family of small reptiles, some with the ability to change color.

Citrus
A tree with fruit that is juicy, with thick skin. They grow in sunny, warm climates, such as Florida. Citrus fruit includes oranges, lemons, limes, and grapefruits.

Civil War
The war fought between the Northern and Southern states from 1861-1865. The Southern states were for slavery. They wanted to start their own country. Northern states fought against slavery and a division of the United States.

Confederacy
The group of 11 Southern states, including Florida, that broke away from the United States during the Civil War. The war lasted from 1861 until 1865.

Ellis Island Congressional Medal of Honor
An award given to "distinguished American citizens who exemplify a life dedicated to community service." The award honors the contributions made by immigrants and their children.

Estuary
The mouth of a freshwater river, where it meets the sea and mixes with saltwater. Estuaries mark the transition zone between river and ocean ecosystems. Many kinds of unique plants and animals live in estuaries.

Huguenots
Members of a French Protestant faith of the 16th and 17th centuries. The Huguenots often fought with French Catholics in the late 1500s and 1600s.

Invasive Species

A plant or animal not normally found in an ecosystem; often introduced accidentally. Invasive species with no natural predators can greatly harm native plants and animals.

Malaria

A serious, sometimes fatal, tropical disease. People get malaria when an infected mosquito bites them.

NASA (National Aeronautics and Space Administration)

A U.S. government agency started in 1958. NASA's goals include space exploration, as well as increasing people's understanding of Earth, our solar system, and the universe. One major NASA facility is the John F. Kennedy Space Center in Florida.

Panhandle

A narrow strip of land that juts out from the rest of the state. Florida's panhandle is made up of the state's 16 westernmost counties.

Peninsula

Land with water on three sides.

Phosphate

A mineral used in fertilizer and food for cattle.

Seminole

Native Americans made up of various Creek Indian tribes and runaway African American slaves who moved into Florida during the 1700s and 1800s.

Swamp

An area that is always wet, usually overgrown with grasses, bushes, and trees.

World War II

A conflict that was fought from 1939 to 1945, involving countries around the world. The United States entered the war after Japan bombed the American naval base at Pearl Harbor, in Oahu, Hawaii, on December 7, 1941.

INDEX

A

Academy Award 28
Ais 18
Alabama 8, 21, 26
Alaska 8
Alligator Alley 34
Animal Kingdom 42
Apalachee 18
Army, U.S. 21, 24
Atlantic Ocean 8, 12, 25

B

Biscayne National Park 43
Britton Hill 8
Busch Gardens 33, 38, 42

C

Calusa 18
Cape Canaveral 39
Caribbean (region) 23, 35
Caribbean Sea 16
Castillo de San Marcos National Monument 25
Central America 16
Cimarrónes 21
Civil War 22
Clearwater, FL 33
Cochran, Jacqueline 28
Colombia 23
Confederacy 22
"Conga" 29
Coppertone 24
Creek 21, 26
Cruise Ship Capital of the World 31
Cuba 10, 23, 29, 31

D

Daytona 500 41
Daytona Beach, FL 41
Daytona International Speedway 41
Defiant Ones, The 28
Douglas, Marjory Stoneman 27
Dry Tortugas 24
Dry Tortugas National Park 24, 43

E

Easter 19
Ellis Island Congressional Medal of Honor 29
Epcot 42
Estefan, Gloria 29
Everglades 4, 10, 11, 17, 24, 26, 27
Everglades National Park 10, 27, 43
Everglades: The River of Grass 27

F

Festival of Flowers 19
Florida A&M University 30
Florida Keys 10, 12, 17, 34
Florida Panthers 40
Florida State University 30
Fort Caroline 20
Fort Jefferson 24
Fort Lauderdale, FL 34
Fort Lauderdale-Hollywood International Airport 35
Fort Matanzas National Monument 25
Fort Moultrie 26
France 20

G

Gasparilla Pirate Festival 33
Georgia 8, 21
Grammy Award 29
Great Britain 20
Green, Benjamin 24
Guess Who's Coming to Dinner 28
Gulf of Mexico 8, 10, 12, 24, 25, 33, 34

H

Haiti 23, 31
Hawaii 8
Hemingway, Ernest 43
Hollywood Studios 42
Huguenots 20

I

In the Heat of the Night 28

J

Jacksonville, FL 20, 32, 41
Jacksonville Jaguars 40
Jacksonville University 32
Jamestown, VA 4

K

Kennedy Space Center, John F. 39, 42
Key West, FL 10, 24, 34, 43
Key West Aquarium 43

L

La Florida 19
Latin America 23
Lightning Capital of the United States, The 25
Lilies of the Field 28

M

Magic Kingdom 42
Major League Baseball 40
Major League Soccer 40
Massachusetts 4
Mel Fisher Maritime Museum 43
Miami, FL 11, 28, 29, 31, 41
Miami Dolphins 40
Miami Gardens, FL 41
Miami Heat 40
Miami Herald 27
Miami International Airport 35
Miami Marlins 40
Miami Sound Machine 29
Minneapolis, MN 27
Minnesota 27
Monticello, FL 12
Mother of the Everglades 27
Museum of Science & Industry 33

N

Naples, FL 34
Narváez, Pánfilo de 20
NASCAR 41
National Basketball Association 40
National Football League 40
National Hockey League 40
New World 18
Nobel Prize 43
North 22

O

Okeechobee, Lake 11
Oklahoma 21, 26
Orange Bowl 41
Orlando, FL 42
Orlando City SC 40
Orlando International Airport 35
Orlando Magic 40
Oscar (award) 28
Osceola 26
Overseas Highway 34

P

Paleo-Indians 18
Palm Beach International Airport 35
Panhandle 8, 30
Pascua Florida 19
Pensacola, FL 28
Poitier, Sidney 28
Ponce de León, Juan 19
Port Everglades 35
Port of Jacksonville 35
Port Miami 35
Port Tampa Bay 35
Presidential Medal of Freedom 27
Puritans 4

Q

Queen of Latin Pop 29

R

Red Hills Horse Trials 30
Red Vet Pet 24

S

Saint Johns River 11
SeaWorld Orlando 38, 42
Seminole 21, 26
Soto, Hernando de 20
South 32
South America 16, 35
South Carolina 21, 26
Spain 19, 20, 21, 25
Sprint Cup Series 41
St. Augustine, FL 4, 19, 20, 25
St. Augustine Alligator Farm Zoological Park 25
St. Petersburg, FL 33
Straits of Florida 10
Sunshine State, The 4, 12
Super Bowl 40

T

Tallahassee, FL 12, 30, 41
Tallahassee Community College 30
Tampa, FL 33, 41, 42
Tampa Bay 33
Tampa Bay Buccaneers 40
Tampa Bay Lightning 40
Tampa Bay Rays 40
Tampa International Airport 35
Tequesta 18
Timucua 18
Titusville, FL 39, 42
To Sir, With Love 28
Tocobaga 18

U

Union 22
United States 10, 15, 20, 21, 22, 23, 24, 25, 26, 28, 32, 35, 37
Universal Orlando Resort 38, 42
University of North Florida 32
U.S. Route 1 34, 43

V

Virginia 4

W

Walt Disney World Resort 38, 42
Wizarding World of Harry Potter 42
World War II 23, 28